Keyword Research Bible
the no. 1 source for keyword research

Contents

Introduction 3
Why is keyword research important? 4
    Starting big, and digging down 5
    Long tail keywords 7
Starting from scratch 9
    Finding your niche market 9
    Uncovering your niche ideas 9
    Testing those ideas 17
    Continuing the niche search 22
    Will this keyword make money? 25
Analyzing the competition 26
    Using free tools 26
No free lunch! 33
    Time or money? 33
    AdSenseAdWords.com 33
    WordTracker 36
    NicheBot 41
    Keyword Analyzer 42
    Spyfu.com 43
You know your business 44
Conclusion 46

Introduction

No matter what kind of business activities you undertake on the internet, there is one fundamental fact that cannot be ignored.

Whether you're promoting internet marketing products, or selling blue widgets from a sales enabled website, you cannot hope to be successful unless people visit your website.

However, having just anybody visit your site is not enough. In order for your business to be successful, you must attract site viewers who are interested in the product or service that you are promoting or selling. In other words, your visitors must be targeted prospects.

For example, if you are the biggest supplier of blue widgets in your locality, it is not going to help your business if everybody who visits your site is only interested in buying red or green widgets.

Similarly, if your site is promoting an internet marketing product that is related to selling on eBay, you're not going to make many sales if the people who visit your site are interested in advanced search engine optimization techniques.

Of course, you do not necessarily want to stop people visiting your site. Even visitors who initially have no interest whatsoever in your product or service may be convinced to do business with you if you have an effective sales page related to a product that they gradually begin to see a use for. However, most of your sales and success will be based upon targeted visitors landing on your site.

Keyword research is fundamentally important to the process of driving targeted visitors to your website. They say that the success of your business ventures online is predicated on how successful you are in your keyword research efforts.

There are many different ways of undertaking effective keyword research. 'The Keyword Research Bible' contains many of them. Many of the methods that you are about to read of are free, and for most people these free tools are more than adequate.

There are, however, some more advanced keyword research resources listed later in this book that will cost you money. However, given the importance of good keyword research to the overall success of your business, any money that you spend on the best tools is always going to represent money well spent.

Why is keyword research important?

Keyword research is all about forcing the search engines to find your website. The vast majority of people who search on the internet do so using search engines like Google or Yahoo!, and you therefore need to make these search engines find your site as often as possible.

Although things are rapidly changing, the search engines are still overwhelmingly text based. In other words, they read the words on the page, and to a large extent they ignore graphics and video.

However, Google in particular is very keen on ranking video materials as well. This is indicative of another important factor about the search engines, which is that they are constantly adapting their practices to match ever-changing markets.

At this moment, however, search engines are overwhelmingly text based search tools, so Flash or Shockwave videos on your site count for nothing with the engines. This despite the fact that your human visitors may love them!

All the major search engines use 'algorithms' to decide how highly they will rate any website that they analyze. Such algorithms are essentially programs (spiders) that can 'read' the words on your page, and then index that particular page based upon what these words tell them the page is about, and how they value it.

A properly constructed webpage will be focused on a particular keyword or phrase. Making sure that this happens is the concern of those who are involved in the art of 'search engine optimization' (SEO).

The first step in the SEO process is to find the keywords or phrases that are going to be most effective for driving targeted traffic to the webpage in question.

Secondly, the webpage will be constructed around that particular keyword or phrase in order to make sure that the search engine 'spiders' realize that this is the phrase you want to be ranked for.

Keyword research must therefore be the most fundamental and vital ingredient of creating a webpage that the search engines will visit, analyze and hopefully love.

When a search engine spider visits your page, it is looking for the most important terms you are using, so that whenever any web searcher types the same term into the search box, the engine shows them your site page. In this way, the search engine helps to send targeted visitors to your site.

It is, therefore, extremely important to use the correct and most appropriate keyword term when building your webpage. Do this, and over time you will be able to drive an increasing number of targeted visitors to your site, and if you are selling a product or service, then you will inevitably increase sales at the same time.

Starting big, and digging down

We have already established that the majority of people who were searching on the internet do so by using a search engine.

There are, however, two different types of searcher:

- The first type is somebody who is just looking for general information and has no specific target or objective in mind. For example, somebody who just wants to learn more about German Shepherd dogs would most probably simply use the phrase 'German Shepherds'. This would do no more than indicate a general broad interest in this particular breed of dog.
- If, however, somebody searched Google or Yahoo using the phrase 'German Shepherd trainer in Kansas', then they have clearly indicated that they have a very specific requirement which they are seeking to satisfy.

    If you happened to be someone who ran a business training German Shepherd dogs in Kansas, you would have every reason to want this particular searcher to visit your website, because you clearly provide exactly the service that they are considering using.

The majority of searchers tend to begin their searching activities using a very broad phrase ('German Shepherds') before progressively narrowing it down to find exactly what they want.

This generally happens because the first search results page that they are presented with does not provide them with the results or the information that they are looking for. They will therefore keep refining the search term that they are using until the search engine shows them the webpages that contain the information that they really want.

For most people who are selling or promoting online, it is unrealistic to expect the search engines to find their website when the searcher is using a very broad generic phrase. This is because the broader the search term is, the more results are going to be returned by the search engine.

For example, using 'German Shepherds' as our search phrase:

Results **1 - 10** of about **983,000** for German Shepherds.

The Google search engine page shows that there are nearly a million results for this particular broad generic term. It is therefore going to be extremely difficult for any new websites to feature on the all-important first page of Google results if they try to do so using this term.

If, however, we were to use a far more specific term, then the result is very different:

> Your search - **"German Shepherd trainer in Kansas"** - did not match any documents.

Clearly, it is not going to be very difficult to be ranked at search position number one for this particular phrase, thereby guaranteeing that anyone looking for a trainer in Kansas on the internet would turn to you.

You might ask whether anybody is actually searching the net using that particular term, and the answer is - apparently not now!

According to Google's statistics, more than 40% of search terms used to query their own search engine every day are brand new. In other words, in every 24 hour period, 40% of searches are run using phrases that nobody has ever searched on before.

This indicates that even if nobody has ever used a particular phrase before, they may well do so in the future.

You should not, of course, build a website around phrases that nobody has ever searched before in the vague hope that they may do so sometime in the future. If you website is your business, then acting in this hopeful (or perhaps hopeless) manner would most probably equate to commercial suicide.

The general point to understand is nevertheless still a valid one. You should not try to compete for the ultra competitive broad generic keywords or phrases, and should focus your attention on finding key words and phrases that are more specific and indicative of potential customers, as opposed to general information seekers.

This is the essence of effective keyword research. Whatever your business is, you need to find the terms and phrases that people use when searching the internet that best indicate that they are a potential customer for your business.

This is what is known as the long tail keyword theory.

Long tail keywords

The principle of the long tail keyword theory is that focusing on driving visitors to your website using broad generic terms is going to be a waste of time. Doing so is extremely unlikely to do anything for your sales.

In other words, the search terms that are most popular are rarely those that will generate the most business for a new (or even a well-established) web site.

It has been demonstrated by many studies that most business is generated from the thousands of website visitors driven by search terms outside the top 30 most popular keyword search phrases.

To take this a stage further, if you added up all the traffic driven by keyword terms and phrases outside the top 30, it would amount to far more visitors than those driven by the phrases that are the most popular.

There also is likely to be far less competition for these long tail phrases, which means that you have far more chance of featuring in the top few results on the search engine pages.

Why it is so important to feature near the top of the search engine results pages? This 'heat map' produced by one of the best-known companies in the 'eye tracking' industry (EyeTools) should answer this question:

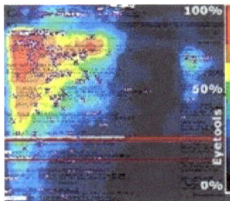

This shows that most people look at the top left-hand side of the search engine results page, which is where the top three to five results are featured.

People's interest then clearly tails off as they move further down the page and over 70% of web searchers never look past the first page of results in any event.

The chances of your site being able to beat 983,000 sites from other webmasters to get into one of the coveted top three places are very slim.

The focus of your keyword research must therefore be on finding long tail keywords with which you have a chance of appearing in the top few results on the first page of Google, Yahoo or MSN.

Starting from scratch

Finding your niche market

If you do not have a web site or business that you want to promote by building one, then you are effectively starting your online money making ventures from a blank piece of paper.

This is not necessarily a bad thing, as it allows you to be flexible and to follow the money. In other words, you are in a position to do your research in order to come up with an idea where you can see that there is money to be made, and then create your site around it.

The first step is therefore to come up with an idea around which you can build your site and your business. This is known as finding your niche market.

We already established that if you build a website based on a broad, generic search term, then it is going to be extremely difficult to generate sufficient quality traffic to make money.

Most marketers will look for niche markets around which to build their monetized website. A niche market of this type is generally a small subcategory of a subcategory of a broader category.

For example, 'dogs' would be very broad category, 'dog collars' would be a subcategory, and 'diamante dog collars' would represent a niche market, wherein people are looking for something very specific.

Results **1 - 10** of about **5,760** for **"diamante dog collars"**.

Any search term that shows less than 10,000 results when run through Google would be a term that would indicate a niche market, one where you have a reasonable chance of getting your site into the first three or four results on the first search results page.

Uncovering your niche ideas

If you have no existing web site and no real idea around what you would like to construct a business, then here is a suggestion that may help to clarify your thinking.

Which is going to be easier to promote and sell? Something that is 'hot' and that everybody wants, or something that nobody has the least interest in?

The answer is obvious, so if you are starting from a blank sheet of paper, then it clearly makes sense to promote a product or service that everybody wants or needs.

While 'diamante dog collars' is clearly a niche topic, a more important question is, how many people are actually searching the internet for such a product?

We can check this very easily using the excellent free keyword research tool at WordTracker:

FREE keyword suggestion tool

Keyword:
diamante dog collars

Adult Filter:
Remove offensive   [Hit Me]

10 Great Reasons to Subscribe to Wordtracker - **Risk-Free!**

No results found for 'diamante dog collars'. Please try again.

As you can see, WordTracker in indicating that they cannot find anybody who is actually searching the net for diamante dog collars. Somebody, somewhere has probably searched this term at some point (I just did, for example!), but what this is really telling you is that there is not enough data to post any meaningful results.

What this means is that you should not attempt to build a whole new niche website based business around this particular search term, as you will probably not receive enough targeted visitors to make it financially worthwhile.

You clearly need to look elsewhere for you niche market idea.

If you can brainstorm your own ideas, then that is always going to be the most effective way of coming up with initial niche suggestions. If you do things in this way, you will naturally come up with ideas that appeal to you, and if something is of interest, then it is going to be far easier (and possibly more enjoyable) to build a website around that particular topic.

So, think about your life, and look around you. Do not discount anything at this stage as potential niche, because you will be amazed at how some online entrepreneurs have managed to build successful niche based sites around seemingly unpromising materials.

Think about what you did yesterday, or what you watched on the TV. How about the stuff in the news and in the papers and magazines? What was the last movie that you watched or the last vacation that you took? What are your hobbies or interests, and how about those of your family (sites that are aimed at youngsters can be hugely successful when they are done right!).

Are there daily tasks that you struggle with, or something where you seem to be uncommonly adept? If so, then why not tell other people about it, and – if it is a problem or a difficulty – tell them how you solved the problem.

The chances are that you are not the only person on the face of planet Earth who has encountered the same difficulty, and, once you start searching the net later, you will be amazed at how many others are searching in the same places for the same information.

Never lose sight of the fact that when people have problems or difficulties, they prefer other people to do their thinking for them! If you can be the one who provides the answers or the solutions, then why not do it?

There really is no way that anybody should find it impossible to come up with a list of twenty or thirty potential niche topics in just a few minutes.

If, however, you do not have a single creative sinew or imaginative gene in your body, there are lots of places you can look at on the net for niche market inspiration.

The first place to visit is the eBay Pulse page, which shows you what is currently selling best and raising the most interest on the world's largest auction site:

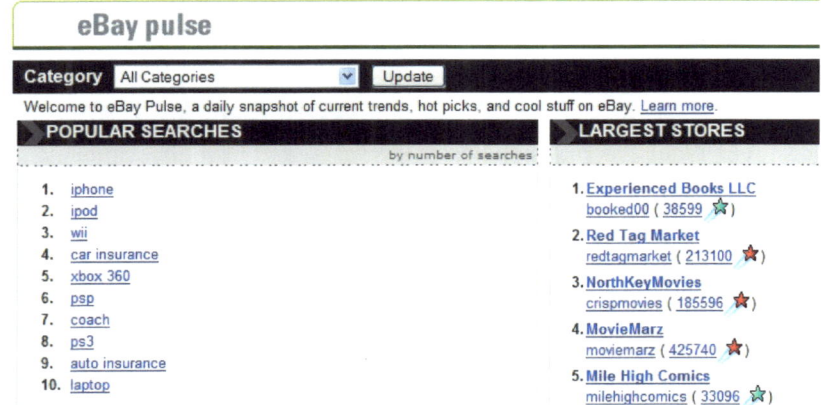

On the left-hand side of the page, you can see the 10 most popular searches on eBay on any given day. This is information that is updated daily.

On the right-hand side of the page, you can see the most popular eBay store sites. These are all popular for a reason, which is that they do their job very well and are therefore a success because of that.

Always be prepared to learn from those who are evidently experts in what they do, as there is never any point in trying to re-invent the wheel. If someone is already doing an excellent job, learn from them rather than trying to start all over again from scratch yourself.

Take a look at the top five stores to see what products they are selling and what kind of promotional materials they are using, because whatever it is that they are doing, it is working.

Looking again at the listing on the left hand side of the page, however, you can see that the iPhone, iPod and the wii are all extremely popular searches at the time of writing.

However, I know from my own experience that these are incredibly competitive market places, and that it is going to be very difficult to find niche markets using these particular products as a guide.

It is not necessarily impossible, just extremely difficult and probably time consuming as well.

The results at number four and number nine are however extremely interesting. Who would have ever thought that anyone would ever look on eBay for car or auto insurance? The very oddity of this would make it something I would investigate further at some time in the future. Not at the moment though, because we still have a niche to find!

Another site that I would visit to get an idea of exactly what people are looking for on the net is Google Trends.

This site shows the hottest terms used to search the world's number one search engine over the last 24 hours.

This page changes literally every day, and therefore you should not make the mistake of trying to build a website around the number one search term, as the chances are very strong that it will not be number one in a couple of days.

The results on the Google Trends page tend to be heavily influenced by current events and what is popular on the TV and on the internet, so I would not necessarily automatically plump for what you see on the first page.

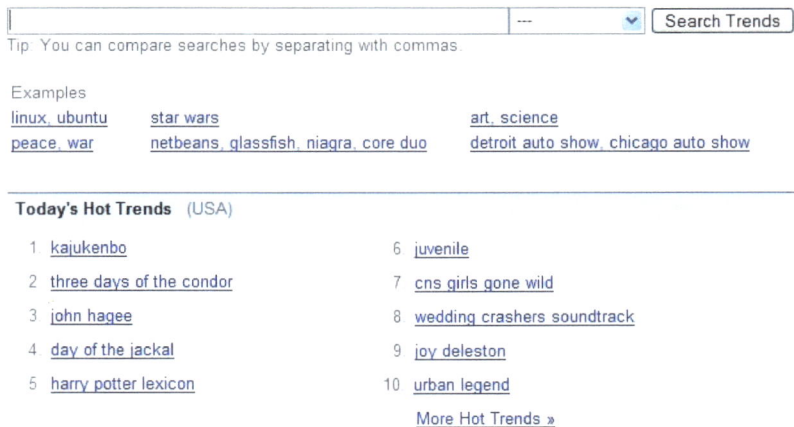

For example, clicking on the most popular hot trend of the day would show you this result:

This clearly indicates that this particular search term has only become popular in the last few hours!

If, however, you were to click on the 'more hot trends' link on the Google Trends homepage, then you would see the top 100 recent searches.

Click on any of the results on this page and you will be shown a very short-term performance chart similar to the one above. This is of little use to you, but try taking any term you are interested in and typing it into the search box at the top of the page as indicated:

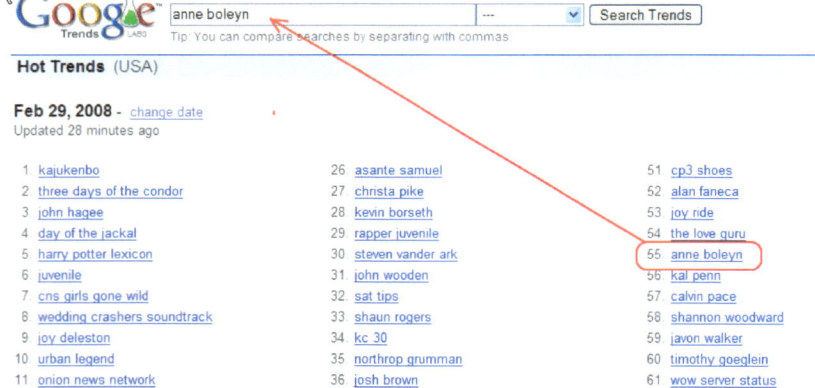

This will give you a much longer-term picture, one that is inherently far more valuable, as it indicates whether there is enough longer term interest in the particular topic to justify building a site around it:

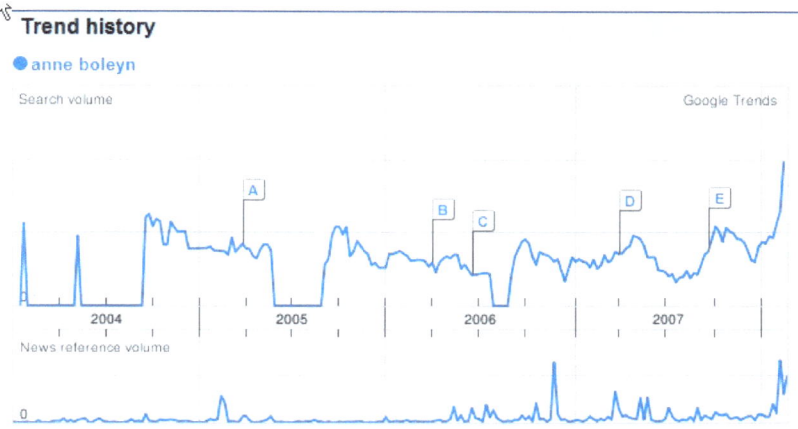

Another great resource for finding new ideas is Amazon.com.

Take a look at the Bestsellers section, whether it is for books or for any of the other items that Amazon sell. This will show you exactly what people want to buy, and, as we have already established, the best business you could ever have is one that sells exactly what people are clamoring to spend their money on.

Books Bestsellers

The Age of Miracles: Embracing the... Hardcover by Marianne Williamson

A New Earth: Awakening to Your Life's... Paperback by Eckhart Tolle

Losing It: And Gaining My Life Back... Hardcover by Valerie Bertinelli

Brisingr (Inheritance, Book 3) Hardcover by Christopher Paolini

› See all bestsellers in Books

The Newest Members of the Apple MacBook Family

 Discover the newest MacBook Airs, MacBooks, and MacBook Pros from Apple. All come pre-loaded with Mac OS X v10.5 Leopard and feature fast Intel Core 2 Duo processors--as well as their own unique features. Order yours from Amazon.com today.

› All new Apple MacBooks

Star Wars Bestsellers

LEGO Trade Federation MTT

LEGO Star Wars Slave I

LEGO® Jedi Starfighter™ with...

LEGO Clone Troopers Battle Pack 7655

› See all bestsellers in Star Wars

If it is a book, look for customer reviews. The more people who have already reviewed it, the more interest that indicates, and the more reason there would be to think about building a site around that topic.

Try reading an excerpt from the book itself.

Is it something that you can empathize with and enjoy? If so, then the chances of your being able to create a site that is genuinely worth visiting and viewing is that much higher.

Remember that coming up with the niche markets that you are eventually going to work with starts with nothing more than an idea.

Hopefully, by now you should be building an ever increasing list of just such ideas. We are not, however, finished with idea generation just yet.

Testing those ideas

Between your own ideas and all of the sites that we have looked at, you should have been able to put together a list of subjects from which you can dig down to try to find suitable niche markets that you can target.

The next step is to move from broad ideas to a focused niche.

I am going to return to eBay to have a look at how we can discover more about the 'xbox 360', and see if there are any possible niche markets lurking underneath that broad phrase.

This keyword on its own is likely to be far too competitive to even think about getting involved in the fight. That should not really need proving – it is self evident - but let's just drive home the point from the main results page of Google. Type 'xbox 360' in and this is the result:

Results **1 - 10** of about **163,000,000** for **"xbox 360"**.

Only 163 million results! It should be a breeze getting into the top three for this particular key phrase then.

More seriously, of course, it is not even worth considering competing with that number of websites.

So, let's go back to the free Wordtracker tool that we used earlier and see what we can discover when we use 'xbox 360' as our 'seed' search term:

xbox 360

29,577 searches (top 100 only)	
Searches	Keyword
9301	xbox 360
5365	xbox 360 cheats
1809	xbox 360 games
1309	xbox 360 elite
420	xbox 360 bundles
314	xbox 360 cheat codes
304	xbox 360 live
268	xbox 360 accessories
255	xbox 360 vs ps3
250	xbox 360 prodam
238	xbox 360 mods
234	xbox 360 release date
223	xbox 360 logo
204	xbox 360 walkthroughs
203	xbox 360 console
203	xbox 360 premium

As you would expect, the number one search term is 'xbox 360', and we already know that trying to compete for this term is a waste of time. So, let's start looking for a good market by working with the second term shown, 'xbox 360 cheats'.

Clearly, with 5365 searches per day this is an extremely popular keyword search. However, this does not mean that you should immediately start building a website around it. Before doing so, you must establish what level of competition you would face if you tried to attract people to your website using this particular keyword search term.

Results 1 - 10 of about 808,000 for "xbox 360 cheats".

Okay, less than a million competing websites. Nevertheless, this would still be far too competitive a term for a new site to become involved in a search engine rankings dogfight.

However, it is still a search term that is generating over 160,000 site visitors every month. The proportion of visitors to websites is therefore reasonable enough to justify further investigation. This is where the really smart keyword researchers start to earn their money.

You can clearly see that people have a massive interest in cheats for the 'xbox 360' gaming system. Now, you need to think about that information laterally, or 'out of the box'.

Firstly, click on the 'xbox 360 cheats' link in the Wordtracker table to see what additional information you can gather:

xbox 360 cheats

6,177 searches (top 100 only)	
Searches	Keyword
5365	xbox 360 cheats
87	free xbox 360 cheats
85	xbox 360 game cheats
25	guitar hero 3 xbox 360 cheats
20	xbox 360 guitar hero 3 cheats
20	xbox 360 oblivion cheats
17	guitar hero 2 xbox 360 cheats
17	turok xbox 360 cheats
17	xbox 360 cheats and codes
17	xbox 360 cheats saints row
12	halo 3 xbox 360 cheats
12	xbox 360 madden online defense cheats

From this you can see that people are particularly interested in learning about free cheats for the 'xbox 360' system. You can also see that they are looking for cheats for particular games.

So, what do you know about specific games for the 'xbox 360' system? Nothing? Me neither, but now is as good a time as any to start learning!

Run a Google or Yahoo! search for 'popular PC games' or 'the most popular PC games'.

When you get your results, check whether the games you're looking at are available for the 'xbox 360'. If they are, then try searching for cheats by using various combinations of the game name, 'xbox 360' and the word 'cheat' or the 'cheats'.

For example, it turns out that one of the most popular games for the 'xbox 360' is currently 'Madden NFL 08'. It is so popular that it even merits its own entry in Wikipedia!

Let's have a look to see if anybody is interested in cheats for this particular game:

Keyword:
madden 08 cheats

Adult Filter:
Remove offensive   [Hit Me]

10 Great Reasons to Subscribe to Wordtracker - **Risk-Free!**

madden 08 cheats

42,016 searches (top 100 only)	
Searches	Keyword
40958	madden 08 cheats
182	madden 08 cheats ps2
171	madden 08 cheats for ps2

Over 40,000 people a day are searching for cheats for this game!

Leaving aside for a moment the question of why anybody would try to cheat while playing a computer game against themselves, let's have a look at the competition for this particular phrase:

Results **1 - 10** of about **65,300** for "**madden 08 cheats**".

So, we have 65,000 websites competing to appear on the first page of the search engine results for a phrase that is generating over 40,000 search requests every day!

This does not necessarily represent a real niche market - there are still too many competing websites and searches being made to genuinely call this a niche.

Nevertheless, I suspect that there is money to be made, simply because so many people out there are looking for cheats for video games.

Furthermore, given the proportion of searchers to websites for Madden 08, it would definitely be a topic around which you could build a moneymaking website page.

Bear in mind that a site or webpage of this nature has inherent disadvantages. If it is successful, it can only ever be so for a short period of time. Madden 08 is going to be replaced by Madden 09 next year, so the maximum life of this page could only ever be one year at the outside.

Video games are a notoriously fast-moving marketplace, and it is therefore highly likely that this game will be replaced by something new even within a few weeks.

That being said, there is probably money to be made at least in the short term, and I am never a fan of walking away from cash! What I would be more inclined to do in this situation is to build a website around 'xbox 360' cheats, and add and/or remove pages when appropriate.

Your 'Madden 08' page could be the focus of your site for as long as it was popular. However, as soon as it was replaced in popular perception by another game and the cheats associated with it then that would be the time to shift the focus of your site.

The main point to take from this is that whenever you find a particular keyword or term that looks like it should be able to earn some money, do not ignore it.

How to make money from such a webpage? Take a look at a digital affiliate network site like Clickbank and see if there are any good 'xbox 360 cheat' related products, or you can attempt to create your own. Otherwise, you could monetize your pages by showing Google AdSense ads and try to generate revenue in this way.

This is not, however, a niche site. It is far too mainstream for one thing. The essential nature of a niche site is that it is something that you can create and promote, and, once it starts pulling visitors and money, walk away from, knowing that it will continue to draw visitors and cash for some time to come.

A site built around Madden 08 cheats could never represent such a thing, but it does nevertheless represent a way of making money from a great keyword, and should not be ignored.

Continuing the niche search

Another great free keyword research tool is NicheBot Classic. Although it actually takes quite a bit of the data it uses from WordTracker (hence we went there first), NicheBot Classic presents it in a slightly different way.

Let's start from a random single term or idea – imagine that we have an interest (fired by any of the resources that we were looking at earlier) in Tibet.

Keyword (click on the ⊕ sign to expand)	100-day count	Predicted daily searches				Competition			Save selected Check all
		Global	Google	Yahoo	MSN	Google	Yahoo	MSN	
tibet ⊕	643	1,134	632	234	108	Check	Check	Check	✓
map of tibet ⊕	82	144	80	29	13	Check	Check	Check	✓
burmese activists join tibet action camp phayul - details ⊕	49	86	47	17	8	Check	Check	Check	✓
free tibet ⊕	47	82	45	16	7	Check	Check	Check	✓

One of the most useful features of Nichebot Classic is its ability to save you time in investigating how much competition there is for a particular keyword or phrase. The figures are listed right there on the right hand side of the page, in the columns shown as 'Check' in this screen shot.

All of the terms shown above are likely to be too competitive, and a quick check confirms this (use the Google competition 'Check' – this is as good a guideline as you need).

However, scrolling a little further down the page, things begin to get a little more interesting:

seven years in tibet ⊕	33	58	32	12	5	Check	Check	Check	☑
tibet authentic goji berries ⊕	29	51	28	10	4	Check	Check	Check	☑
tibet authentic ⊕	26	45	25	9	4	Check	Check	Check	☑

Goji berries?

It seems like quite a few folks are interested in them, and I would guess that the second result for 'tibet authentic' is a spin-off from the first one as well, so NicheBot is predicting a combined total of nearly 100 searches per day between the two phrases.

Let's take a look at what more we can learn about Goji berries, and how many other people want to know about them:

There are a few things to note here:

- First, there are only 1520 searches for 'tibet authentic goji berries'. That is exactly the sort of number that screams 'niche market' at you.
- Second, the top result on the left hand side of the page is from Amazon.com! That means that you could earn money by selling these berries from Amazon as an associate (affiliate), generating a commission by doing so.

That would not necessarily be the way that I would recommend making money from Goji berries, however, especially as Amazon will only pay you a measly 4% commission. You are going to have to sell a few truckloads of berries to make a decent living at that rate!

Another thing that you can see from the snapshot of the Google search page is that there is an advert featured on the right hand side of the page. This tells you that someone believes there is enough money to be earned from advertising on a search engine results page that is concerned with Goji berries to pay money to try it out.

Note that I say 'someone believes' that there is money to be made.

Too often, you will read advice that seeing advertising of this nature categorically tells you that there is money to be made from this advertising. It does not. That advert could have been placed there yesterday as a marketing test, and the person who created it could simply be seeing whether they can make money from their ad or not.

However, even this has one great advantage for you. You can let them test the water for you. Keep an eye on this page for a week or so, and see what happens. If the same ad is still there after that, then you know that there is money being made from it, and that should help to firm up your ideas about creating an appropriate website.

It might also indicate that you should advertise yourself once your site has gone live to generate an initial surge of traffic.

If the ad is gone, however, then maybe the situation is not so clear, although the reason that they were not making money (and therefore pulled the ad) could be the result of many possible variables (poor ad copy, badly targeted advertising, etc).

The next step if this is a totally new subject for you is to do your research. It turns out that Tibetan Goji berries are supposed to be a wonder health food that is rich in antioxidants, amino acids and vitamins, so there is absolutely no reason why we should not be promoting them.

Do we build a site exclusively based on Goji berries or not?

If you are able to find a way to sell Goji berries themselves and make a profit by doing so, then there is absolutely no reason why you should not do so.

The potential downside of this is that you are focusing all of your efforts on one single product, and the fact that there are only 1500 sites on the net referencing Goji berries at the moment tells you that it is still a very small market at present.

The (more sensible) alternative would be to create a natural health site, and make Goji berries a featured topic by creating a page specifically referencing them.

Would that be an effective money maker?

Will this keyword make money?

We have already established that the secret of making money is getting your site or page found when someone runs a search, and that in order to do so, you need to appear in the first three to five results on the first search engine results page.

The search engine spiders are pretty lazy creatures, because they assume (quite rightly) that humans are all the same! They like sites to have a name (the URL) that tells them exactly what it is about, and the more clearly the name spells out the message, the better.

Having a site that carries the keyword that you want to rank for in the URL is therefore a major plus point as far as Google, Yahoo! and MSN are concerned. That generally means that it is going to be easier to rank highly for that particular keyword phrase.

So, 'tibet-authentic-goji-berries.com' would be a great domain name, as it contains the exact primary keyword that you are trying to rank for. This would, however, drastically restrict the focus of your site to the one product, and there may not be enough money in the Goji berry market to justify that at present.

The alternative is to create just one page of your site to promote the benefits of Goji berries.

In this case, the site may be called 'best-natural-health.com' and the page Title would then be 'tibet-authentic-goji-berries'. Thus, the URL of this specific page would be 'best-natural-health.com/ tibet-authentic-goji-berries', and this would still be a powerful enough indicator to the search engines as to what the page is about.

The rest of the best-natural-health site could be built around other keywords that related to other natural products.

Analyzing the competition

Using free tools

Once you have found an appropriate niche related keyword phrase and decided how you are going to construct your site, the next thing to do is to study and analyze your competition, because there is a lot that you can learn by doing so. You do this for two reasons:

- Given that your objective is to get into the top three search engine results quickly, you need to know how difficult this will be.
- You cannot hope to make a profit from just one keyword phrase. You need to have other keyword phrases driving visitors to different pages of your site, so you need to build a list of such words as quickly and easily as possible. The simplest way of doing this is borrowing keyword phrases from other websites!

The first thing that you should look at is the Google Page Rank of the pages that appear at the top of the search engine rankings.

Google PR is a measure of how highly rated any particular page is by Google and, as that is the #1 search engine that you are striving to be ranked by, PR carries a great deal of significance.

Head on over to the excellent SEO Chat site and use the Page Rank Checker to see what kind of results you are going to be up against.

In the first instance, sort the page by 'Page Rank' as shown below:

PageRank Results — tibet authentic goji berries
Order by (pagerank) | Results (10) | Search

Showing **search results** in order of **pagerank**   **17,100** results found

Amazon.com: Tibet Authentic Goji Berries, 16-Ounce Bag (Pack of 2 ...
4/10
Amazon.com: Tibet Authentic Goji Berries, 16-Ounce Bag (Pack of 2): Grocery.
http://www.amazon.com/Tibet-Authentic-Goji-Berries-16-Ounce/dp/B000KPXAHK
View META Data - View Inbound Links - Analyze Links
Cached Version - Similar Web Sites

GojiBerry.com, the **Tibetan Goji Berries** site, retail, wholesale ...
3/10
To find a vendor selling authentic Tibetan Goji berries and Goji berry products in your area The Tibetan Goji Berry Company. ...
http://www.gojiberry.com/
View META Data - View Inbound Links - Analyze Links
Cached Version - Similar Web Sites

Alissa Cohen Raw Food Store :: Food :: **Authentic Tibetan Goji** ...
3/10
These are the authentic, pure goji berries that are shade dried, organically cultivated wild plants. These Tibetan goji berries have been grown in protected ...
http://www.alissacohen.com/shop/product.php?cat=0&page=1&productid=7
View META Data - View Inbound Links - Analyze Links
Cached Version - Similar Web Sites

Raw Wild Organic **Tibet Authentic Goji Berries** - 6.6 lbs ...
3/10
Tibetan Goji Berries are actually grown in Tibet. All other "Tibetan Goji Berries" available are actually Tibetan varieties of the Goji Berry that...
http://www.rawguru.com/store/raw-food/raw_wild_tibet_authentic_goji_berries.html
View META Data - View Inbound Links - Analyze Links
Cached Version - Similar Web Sites

Amazon.com: Tibet Authentic Goji Berries, 8-Ounce Bag (Pack of 3 ...
2/10
Amazon.com: Tibet Authentic Goji Berries, 8-Ounce Bag (Pack of 3): Grocery.
http://www.amazon.com/Tibet-Authentic-Goji-Berries-8-Ounce/dp/B000KPV6GM
View META Data - View Inbound Links - Analyze Links

The top result (which is the page highlighted earlier from Amazon.com) ranks a 4/10. After that, it immediately drops away to a handful of 3/10 results and than 2/10.

None of these results should represent any major cause for concern, because competing against pages ranked relatively low in this manner indicates that you should be able to achieve a top ten ranking within a few weeks.

You should then run the same test, but sort the pages according to relevance. That will show you the pages that are most closely related to the search term that you have input, which is indicative of the sites that represent your closest competition for this exact search phrase.

Incidentally, there is a whole heap of excellent free tools available on the SEO Chat site. Make sure that you bookmark it, because it is one of the most useful sites around when it comes to building your keyword lists.

You have established that getting your site onto the first page of the Google search results for this particular search phrase is not likely to be too difficult.

The next thing to look at is what other keywords you can find that you can use to drive visitors to your site.

Go back to the free WordTracker or NicheBot keyword search tools and run a search for 'Goji berries':

goji berries

722 searches (top 100 only)	
Searches	Keyword
434	goji berries
52	organic goji berries
46	tibet authentic goji berries
38	tibetan goji berries wholesale
28	dried goji berries
15	himilayan goji berries
7	chocolate covered goji berries
7	goji berries health benefits
7	health benefit of goji berries
7	sprouting goji berries
6	dried goji berries free shipping
6	heaven mountain goji berries

There are quite a few more interesting search terms there, so check the competition and, if the phrase looks like it might work (some searches and not too many competitors), add it to your 'Goji berry' list.

Look at the excellent free Google Suggest tool. This program acts like the predictive text feature that you see on many mobile phones. The tool tries to tell you other phrases that it finds from the Google database that are linked to what you are typing in, and gives you the number of pages that it finds as well:

We have already established that anything with less than 10000 searches is a valid term to work with, so there are a few other phrases that you can work with here.

Take anything that you find from Google Suggest and dig deeper by searching on that phrase too. 'Goji juice scam' looks like it would be worth investigating further, both for information that could be used on your webpages, and keywords.

Next, go back to your earlier SEO Chat Page Rank results and grab the URL of a couple of the top sites that you saw (don't bother with Amazon.com, incidentally – it will probably not work for what we are going to do next).

Look up Spyfu.com. Paste the URL into the box on the home page as shown, and click through to see what results you get.

Even the free version of this site basically allows you to 'spy' on your competition, hence its name. However, when you type in the site name, make sure that you do not include the 'http://www.' part of the domain name – do so, and you are not going to get any results shown!

Scroll down the page and on the left hand side you can see some of the other keyword search terms that this site is attempting to rank for, and beneath that are listed the top competitors' sites:

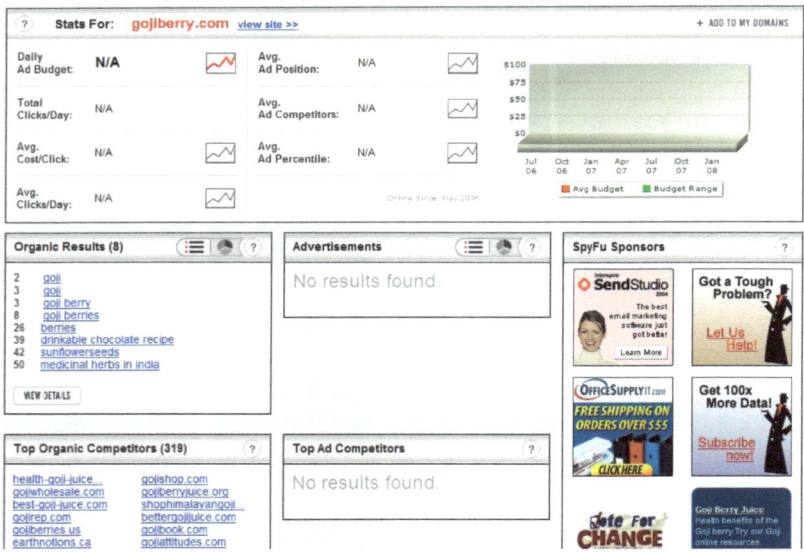

You can now take each of these sites in turn and see what keywords they are using in order to achieve search rankings too.

Spyfu also tells you that this particular site des not appear to be spending any money on advertising.

Nevertheless, if you take a look at the Google AdWords Keyword Tool, you will also get an in-depth analysis of all of the search terms that this site is using, although (in this particular case) there is no data about what the competition is like:

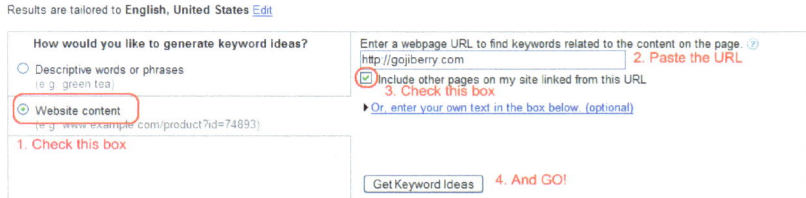

Here are the first twenty results, with an indication of search volumes:

Another excellent tool for finding out about the competition is QuantCast, which carries data about over 20 million websites! Even for those for which it does not have accurate data, it still makes an estimate, which is extremely valuable information:

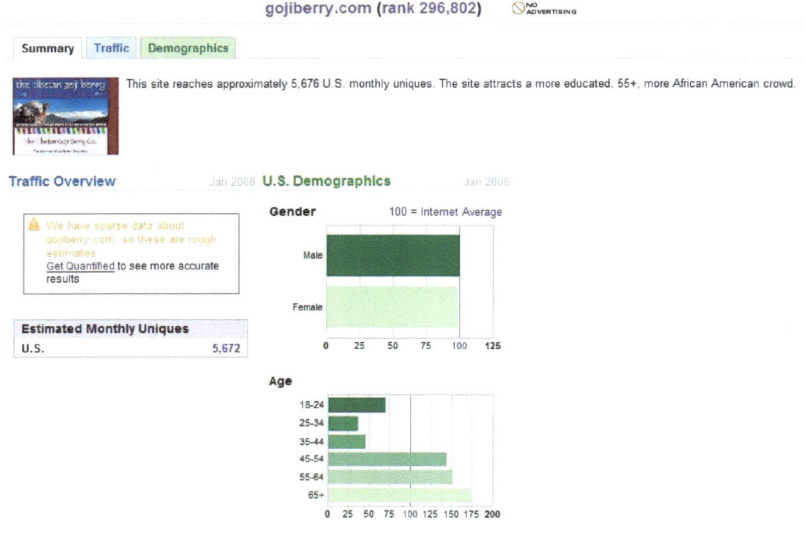

This is super-targeting data. It is telling you that, according to their best estimate (which I believe is based on the 'Rank' shown at the top of the page), this competitor site receives 5672 unique visitors a month, and that the main visitors are likely to be a well educated, mainly Afro-American audience of over 55's.

If you do not already know the answer, this information will certainly help you to decide whether the product that you want to offer to your target audience is going to work or not.

Knowing the number of visitors that a direct competitor enjoys also enables you to assess whether a page that you create is likely to make money for you.

Given that your intention is to surpass this competitor's results, knowing how many visitors they enjoy should give you a clear indication of how many people are likely to visit your site in a few months time as well.

No free lunch!

Time or money?

The tools that we have been using so far cost you nothing in monetary terms, but what they do cost you is time. There can be little doubt that they are relatively labor intensive.

You know that effective keyword research is fundamental to the success of your site, so you must do everything that you can to make sure that you do the job correctly. This may well involve making payments.

Here are some of the best paid keyword research sites:

AdSenseAdWords.com

AdSenseAdWords features a list of the best paying keywords according to Google's AdWords advertising program.

Basically, as the descriptive name might imply, if you are using a Pay Per Click advertising program like AdWords, then every time someone clicks on your ad, you pay.

It follows that the more expensive a keyword phrase is when using AdWords, the more difficult it is likely to be drawing traffic to your site using that term or phrase.

To get some idea of just how difficult:

VITAL STATISTICS

Updated Weekly

Number of keywords: 580765

Over 10c:	466713
Over 15c:	451850
Over 25c:	421936
Over 50c:	351351
Over $1:	251488
Over $5:	50177
Over $10:	20629
Over $20:	6240
Over $50:	179

This tells you that there are 179 keyword phrases that advertisers are willing to pay over $50 per click for.

Remember that this is not for a new customer sign-up or even someone agreeing to join a mailing list. This is over $50 every time someone actually looks at the advert in question!

It is somewhat hard to believe that anyone can really be making money when their advertising is so expensive, but that must be the case, otherwise they would not be doing it.

Position	Keywords	Cost/Click	clicks/day	Date Added	up/down/same?	Google Link
1	california mesothelioma attorneys	101.26	0	12/19/2007		Search Google
2	california mesothelioma lawyers	90.17	0	12/19/2007		Search Google
3	attorney county dui orange	83.05	1			Search Google
4	colorado truck accident lawyer	82.45	0	12/11/2007		Search Google
5	call conference pricing	81.47	0	12/22/2005		Search Google
6	call conference vendor	80.1	0	12/22/2005		Search Google
7	colorado truck accident attorney	76.13	0	12/11/2007		Search Google
8	attorney diego law lemon san	75.22	1			Search Google
9	county dui lawyer orange	73.62	1			Search Google
10	blood cord donating umbilical	72.18	1			Search Google
11	austin dwi	71.61	5			Search Google
12	atlanta auto accident attorney	70.77	1			Search Google
13	california mesothelioma attorney	70.77	1	12/19/2007		Search Google
14	auto accident lawyer ny	69.45	1			Search Google
15	[peritoneal mesothelioma]	69.27	1			Search Google

So, is there anyone paying to advertise anything that is Goji related, and, if so, how much are they willing to pay?

	Date Added	Keyword	Cost/Click	Clicks a Day	Google Link
1.	11/16/2005	goji juice	2.76	18	Search Google
2.	11/16/2005	himalayan goji juice	2.54	2	Search Google
3.		organic goji berries	2.12	1	Search Google

This shows that there is over $2 being paid per click for all three Goji related terms that are currently being paid for on the AdWords site.

That would indicate that there is money being made by the sites that are advertising using these terms. After all, over $2 per click is not cheap unless the conversion rates are justifying the spending.

You already know who the target audience is for this particular product from QuantCast. Now you can also see that there are advertisers willing to pay to promote their products to these people.

34

This program is an excellent tool for additional research purposes, because it indicates the main keyword phrases for your product, and highlights how expensive it is going to be should you choose to invest in paid advertising at some later time yourself.

The importance of such advertising is that it represents the quickest and simplest method of driving traffic to your site and is therefore something that you may want to consider.

What you should do now is check who is paying for advertising using these phrases.

```
Results 1 - 10 of about 571,000 for goji juice. (0.59 seconds)

                        Sponsored Links

        Goji ?
        Before You buy Goji. Read This !
        Learn How I Make $10,000 Per Month
        internetmilliondollarexposed.com

        台灣的頂尖商機
        賺大錢! 具有完善的新系統
        直銷史上發展最快的公司現已在台灣開
        www.X1Concept.com

        Noni Juice Pure Direct
        Flown in daily for freshness
        All your health issues answered
        NoniPureJuice.com

        Join Xango
        Awesome Product
        Amazing Earning Potential
        Ready2goXango.com
```

Take the URL of each of these sites in turn and run it through the tools that we looked at earlier. This should enable you to discover exactly what keyword phrases are being used to send people to Goji berry related websites by the businesses behind these sites.

The best news about AdSenseAdWords is that there is a free trial available at the moment which I would definitely recommend that you should take advantage of. Doing so obviously presents an ideal opportunity for you to test this excellent tool out to see how you can use it in the future.

WordTracker

We have already established that the free version of WordTracker is an excellent tool. The paid version, however, takes that performance and power up several notches.

In order to test the usability of the paid WordTracker version, it is possible to take advantage of the free trial that they offer, but be warned. It is only functional for two hours after they send you the activation link, so be ready to go before your apply!

Let us imagine that we want to search for keywords related to acne.

In the full paid version, you open up the 'Keyword Universe' utility of the site and go from there, but in the free trial version, just type the base keyword into the first screen box:

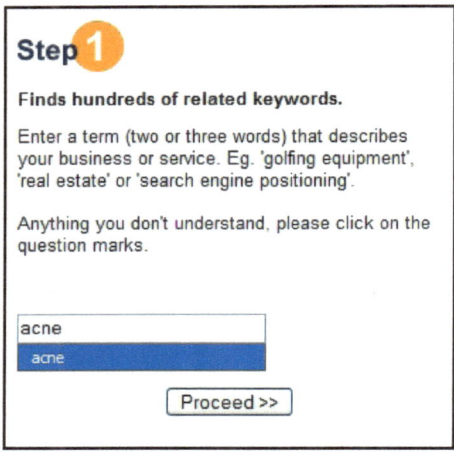

and hit 'Proceed'.

The first thing that you have is the table on the left hand side of the page. Click on the top word 'acne' and the table on the right then appears.

In this trial, you are allowed to add up to 30 words to the basket of key phrases that you are going to analyze.

However, at the bottom of the page (beneath the right hand table) there is a note that tells me that there are another 85 results for this particular word.

Click on any words from the right hand table that you want to analyze to add them into your 'basket' of 30 words:

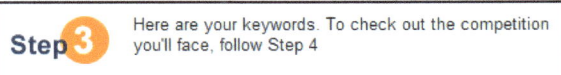

Click here for step 4

Total number of keywords you selected : 31		
Keyword	Count	Remove
acne	1367	Delete
acne cream treatment	610	Delete
acne treatment	480	Delete
acne cream differin	427	Delete
acne cream retina	415	Delete
acne cream	385	Delete
acne scars cream	323	Delete
proactive acne cream	292	Delete

Click straight through to 'step 4' as indicated:

BEST SEARCH TERMS FOR MSN

Msn gets 9.0000% of all search engine traffic (approx. 45 million a day).

What do these headings mean? Click here

No.	Keyword Why quotes?	KEI Analysis (?)	Count (?)	24Hrs (?)	Competing (?)
1	"acne cream retina"	499.203	415	59	345
2	"how do i get rid of old acne scars"	368.000	184	26	92
3	"acne cream treatment"	269.638	610	87	1380
4	"acne cream differin"	172.008	427	61	1060
5	"acne scars cream"	159.769	323	46	653
6	"proactive acne cream"	101.024	292	42	844
7	"acne scarring tissue treatments"	15.754	31	4	61
8	"california acne treatment"	11.607	65	9	364
9	"acne dermatology treatment"	5.594	70	10	876

What you see in the free trial is the results taken from MSN which, as WordTracker points out, represent 9% of the market.

The main thing that makes WordTracker so valuable is the KEI Analysis figures shown in the table. This is automatically doing what we were doing manually earlier by taking a keyword term and checking how many sites there were for it in the Google search engine results (although WordTracker is using the much smaller and therefore less authoritative MSN, rather than Google).

The top term shown is 'acne cream retina'. What the figures then tell you is that the predicted number of web searchers who are likely to use that phrase in a 24 hour period is 59 and that there are total of 345 sites listed on MSN that are related to that search term.

Hence, the KEI Analysis figure (effectively representing one divided by the other) is 499.

You do not need to know exactly how his figure is calculated or what it actually means. The important thing is that WordTracker suggest that any search term with a KEI figure of over 10 is a good keyword to use, so basically the top 8 terms here are all valuable and worth trying to draw site visitors with.

Your trial results have been filtered to remove adult words.

Keyword (?)	Count (?)	Predict (?)	Dig (?)
acne cream treatment	610	968	
acne treatment	480	762	
acne treatments	217	344	
acne scar treatment	136	216	
acne laser treatment	115	183	
laser acne treatments	111	176	
home treatment for acne	101	160	
acne_treatments	98	156	
best acne treatment	98	156	
acne home treatment	78	124	

Another terrific thing that you can do in the full version of WordTracker is 'dig down' deeper when you find a phrase that you believe you can use, to see what other keywords are 'buried' beneath it.

We can take a look at what is 'hidden' under the phrase 'acne cream treatment', for example, simply by clicking on 'Dig'.

Keyword (?)	Count (?)	Predict (?)	Dig (?)
acne cream treatment	610	968	
acne rosacea forums acne cream gel sever acne treatments and	5	8	
bleaching cream for acne scar treatment	4	6	
clean 26 clear blackhead clearing acne treatment cream	4	6	
natural skin care cream acne treatment	4	6	
new acne treatment cream wrinkle	4	6	

Now we are really getting some great long tail keyword phrases.

While there are not huge numbers of people searching for them, what you would do is try to create a site page that was optimized for several of these search terms.

Using the full paid version of WordTracker allows you to build a massive list of keywords, and using the KEI Analysis figures gives you a very clear idea of which phrases you have a chance of making money with.

That's all of the good news – WordTracker is a terrific search tool - so I would definitely recommend that you take the free trial and 'play' with it. That is obviously he best way of discovering just how powerful it is.

Now, the bad news. WordTracker is not cheap, or more accurately there are keyword research tools on the market that will cost you less.

Good keyword research is the single main factor behind having a successful online business, so no matter what it costs, the best keyword research tools are always cheap!

Annual subscription (Our best value – one year minimum term)	$329 USD	Buy now
	£165 GBP	Buy now
Monthly subscription (One month minimum term)	$59 USD	Buy now
	£29 GBP	Buy now
One week subscription	$30 USD	Buy now
	£15 GBP	Buy now

There is really very little risk with WordTracker anyway, as there is a 30 day money back guarantee. What I would therefore suggest if you are planning to use WordTracker is to use the free trial and the free tool that we looked at earlier.

Use them in combination to put together an initial list of keywords and phrases for whatever niche it is that you are interested in.

Then take a subscription for a week and spend the whole seven days doing nothing other than researching keywords and phrases using WordTracker.

Make sure that everything is prepared before you start, and aim for at least five or six thorough searches per day. Do that and you should have enough materials to go on for the next three months, and then you can do the same thing once again.

NicheBot

One of the best features in the paid version of NicheBot is that it draws its keyword research data from several sources, amongst which is our friend WordTracker.

In fact, the paid NicheBot claims to allow you to search three of the major keyword databases and that doing so gives you access to 295 billion keywords!

As a new version of the program has just been recently launched, it also has all of the latest keyword research technology already included.

For example, Google are putting a lot of focus on 'LSI', which is short for Latent Semantic Indexing. The idea behind this concept is that there are some words that naturally go together, and that the spider can assess how naturally a site has been constructed by reference to this 'twinning concept'.

If your site was about tables, then it would be natural that chairs would be mentioned a few times on your pages. The Google spider will search for this term and take finding it as a positive sign, whereas not finding it would represent a negative.

LSI is becoming increasingly important and NicheBot is the first keyword site that I am aware of that is already including it in their search options.

There is also the ability to filter the keywords and phrases that you discover through NicheBot using 16 different filtering criteria, and there is also an excellent video based training library to enable you to get started using the program effectively the moment you subscribe.

In terms of the cost, NicheBot is a site that you pay monthly, and there are two different levels of membership available, both of which are based on a system of credit that you buy (which never expires, so that any credits that you do not use are automatically carried forward for as long as you remain a member).

The 'Lite' version of the program costs $13.97 per month (equivalent to only $0.46 per day) While the 'Avid' version, for the more serious keyword researcher, is priced at $27.97.

Both versions of the program have a 14 day trial that will only cost you $1.00, during which time you can do a awful lot of effective keyword research! You should take advantage of this excellent offer to discover more about what NicheBot has to offer!

Given that all of the WordTracker data is available through NicheBot this would definitely be my paid keyword research tool of choice.

Keyword Analyzer

Keywords Analyzer is another excellent paid for program, one feature of which I particularly like and use regularly.

Once you have built your keyword list, then you want to know as much as you can about the validity of the terms that you have gathered.

In order to do this, you could take each query term and head over to Google to check how many competitor sites there are manually, or you can use Keyword Analyzer to do the job for you automatically.

Before doing this, you should make sure that your list is cleaned of duplicates and so on. There is an excellent free tool on the SEO Tools site that this will do this job for you, as well as removing 'bad' keywords and those that are primarily numbers based.

Once the list is cleaned, set Keyword Analyzer to work, and it will go and find all of the Google competitive information for every phrase on your site, no matter how many of them there are.

One note of caution, however. Google do not always like it if you start bombarding their site with thousands of information requests, and have been known to ban people from using their site because of it, albeit only for a few days.

When you are running a massive Google research campaign, you should set it up using an anonymous proxy server of the kind that you will find here. If this does not make a great deal of sense to you because you are not sure what a proxy server is and what it does, take a look at Wikipedia for the answers.

Keyword Analyzer is a one-off purchase that will cost you $97.

Spyfu.com

Like most of the other tools highlighted above, while using the free version of Spyfu gives you access to some excellent information, using the paid version allows you to 'spy' on your competitors so much more quickly and efficiently.

For example, while using the free version enables you to see a brief snapshot or the organic search terms that your competitors are using, and shows you who the main competition are, the paid version gives you hundreds or sometimes even thousands of the keywords that other sites are using.

It also gives you many more data 'levels' so that you can dig down deeper into the sites that you want to 'spy' on to see what makes them effective.

This is obviously information that is extremely pertinent to you, because once you know how other people are able to create sites that are efficient money making machines, it becomes much easier for you to do the same!

If you are not sure about whether spyfu.con is going to be useful to your business, then you can subscribe for as little as three days for $6.75, so that is what I would do so that you can get a taste of the real power of being able to spy on your main competition.

You know your business

So far, we have looked at how you go about building a monetized web site from a standing start, a position where all you know is that you want to start earning money online.

However, maybe you are in the position of already knowing exactly what the topic of your site is going to be, either because you already have a pre-existing business or have already come up with a terrific idea around which you want to construct your site.

In this case, you are going to skip a lot of the niche finding that we did earlier on and dive straight into putting together the keyword list that is going to drive targeted visitors to your website.

We have already looked at a handful of the best there is to offer in both paid and free keyword research tools, and the keyword research methods that I have worked through in this book will apply just as much to your situation as they do to any other.

However, before using these tools, I would recommend that you start from a slightly different perspective. Begin by using a vastly underutilized method of discovering keywords or phrases that you can use to bring people to your sales enabled website.

If you have a website selling a product or service, then it is a reasonable assumption that you know a significant amount about the product or service that you are promoting.

The first thing you should do to start generating a keyword list is, therefore, simply to brainstorm and use your own knowledge to start building your list.

If, for example, you are selling diamante dog collars, then it is a fair assumption that you will know considerably more about them than 99% of the population.

Who could be better positioned to come up with some basic keyword phrases than you?

The temptation is to simply let computer technology do all the work for you, but I would suggest that if you do, then you are shortchanging both yourself and your business. No matter how smart or intuitive it may be, no computer program could ever know your business as well as you do.

At this point in your keyword research, you should not try to second-guess internet searchers by trying to come up with phrases that you think people might use to search for your product or service. Instead, what you should do is try to come up with key words and phrases that you yourself would use if you were a reasonably knowledgeable potential customer for your product.

For example, if I was considering buying a diamante dog collar, I would be interested in whether such a thing would be good for my dog, or not. I might therefore come up with the phrase 'benefits of diamante dog collars'.

At this stage, I would not be overly concerned as to whether this was a realistic search term, as we will be filtering and eliminating many possible keyword search phrases later on in the process of building a viable and valuable keyword list.

So, grab a pen and paper or open up a text editor on your PC and just write down every phrase or term you can think of that could possibly relate to your product or service. The more terms or phrases you can come up with, the better.

Let's say that you come up with 50 phrases or terms. That represents a great start, and only after that should you start using computers to do the work for you

Conclusion

The ability to conduct effective and thorough keyword research is a basic, fundamental skill that any serious online marketer or entrepreneur must acquire.

Without a good keyword list, there is little or no chance that you will ever be able to drive targeted, focused prospects from free organic searches, which will in turn condemn you to paying for every lead that you ever get.

Natural, organic search results are becoming a more important factor on the net every day as more and more searchers use them in preference to the paid adverts that the search engine results pages feature.

Go back to the 'heat map' that we looked at very early in this book if you want to see conclusive proof of this fact. The red hot part of the page is very firmly focused on the top left hand side, because that is exactly where the vast majority of searchers look when they are first presented with a results page.

You are bound to miss out on the vast majority of your best and most targeted traffic if you cannot appear on the search engine results pages for those search terms that are most appropriate to your product or services.

You can only hope to feature in the top three to five results if you build your site around suitable long tail keywords and phrases, that is, those that enjoy some visitors but do not show too much competition.

It is therefore no exaggeration to say that the long term success of your business depends on you acquiring the skills and tools that will enable you to do you keyword research properly.

This book teaches you the methods that you need to apply in order to gain those skills and shows you where you can find the resources and tools so that you are able to do the job properly.

'The Keyword Research Bible' gives you everything you need to be an ultra-successful keyword researcher, starting right now.

www.ingramcontent.com/pod-product-compliance
Lightning Source LLC
Chambersburg PA
CBHW040925180526
45159CB00002BA/621